CW00839491

"A big thank you to Ian Harm who has been a close friend and for all his valuable advice given over the years which has helped keep me firmly on the right side of the law!"

Ray Castlehow

So you want to be a...
Private Investigator

Ray Castlehow & Rick Armstrong

Fisher King Publishing
The Studio, Arthington Lane,
Pool-in-Wharfedale,
LS21 1JZ,
England.

So you want to be a Private Investigator

Copyright © Ray Castlehow & Rick Armstrong 2012

ISBN 9781479227655

All rights reserved. No part of this publication may be
reproduced or distributed in any form or by any means, or
stored in a database or retrieval system, without the prior
written permission of Fisher King Publishing.

So you want to be a...
Private Investigator

Ray Castlehow & Rick Armstrong

Ray Castlehow served 13 years in the Royal Air Force in Mechanical Transport. After leaving the RAF he specialised in Road Traffic Accident Investigation. Over several years Ray established his reputation throughout the insurance and legal industries. In 2005 he started North by North West Investigations Ltd.

The company has continuously expanded its UK operations to offer a broad range of Private Investigation services alongside its work within the insurance industry on liability and accident fraud cases. In recent years it has grown its commercial investigations portfolio.

Ray presents regularly on the topic of Insurance Fraud Investigation. He has written and directed a training DVD to clearly show how staged accidents occur and he is working with the insurance industry and leading developers to launch mobile applications to further assist with vehicle accident fraud prevention.

Rick Armstrong has a background in management consultancy, advertising, training and marketing. For two decades he worked in the Middle East.

For a time Rick was CEO of a law firm specialising in the laws surrounding the Regulation of Investigatory Powers Act, the European Convention on Human Rights, Covert Policing and Anti-Terrorism.

Rick has several business interests, he is the founder of Mentor Group, Director of IQ Property Investments, MD of Pixel Vector Apps and Area Director of BNI. He is an inspirational speaker regularly presenting on topics such as business creation, motivation and leadership skills. He is co-author of The Little Book of Positive Thoughts, The Little Book of Visualisation and the Little Book of Philosophy.

So you want to be a Private Investigator. Why? It could be that you work in a similar field in the police or the military and the possibility of working for yourself in the private sector is an attractive proposition. Maybe you are looking for a career change and this is something that you believe you could do. Then there are those who want to get into this industry because of the works of fiction that portray the world of the 'gumshoe' as something that is exciting and edgy with bragging rights to impress their partner, family or friends... If that last one is you, may we suggest you look for a career elsewhere.

So long as the reason you want to be a PI is based on a realistic approach to the opportunities that exist and that you have done your due diligence so that you are making your decision based more on knowledge than gut instinct, then this could well be the right choice for you.

But before you get your business cards printed and stick an advertisement in the local paper in the hope that business will simply come to you, understand that before all else you need business skills to make this work. What do you know about marketing, business planning, sales initiatives, referral networking, brand strategies, web design, social media and finance? If asked to make a presentation to the senior partners of a law firm or an insurance company to pitch for their business, do you know where to start? How will you establish your credibility? If you have to write a detailed report describing a complex surveillance operation that could be used as evidence in a legal case, are you confident of your skill in getting it right?

There is a lot to consider before starting any business but being a PI can carry with it its own unique set of complications. In this book we have not set out to write a definitive guide but simply to highlight points to take on board which might help to give you direction toward seeking more information before you leap into what can be a great career in a form of work that is ever changing and always challenging.

You are not a spy so don't act like one. Leave James Bond in the pages of fiction. You are providing a professional service for clients who are placing their trust in you so be professional at all times.

Research other agencies in your area to understand as much about their business as you can find out. What services do they offer? Are they specialists in a particular area of work or are they generalists? What is their pricing structure? How many staff do they have? Are they a small local firm or part of a larger National franchise? Look for those to whom you could refer work and there is a strong chance they will reciprocate.

Private Investigators have no more authority than any ordinary citizen and that includes in matters of traffic law. Do not take the law into your own hands and do not act as if you represent the law.

You are not a magician. You are in an industry which revolves around detail and observation. This detailed information is generated through diligence, knowing where to look and who to speak with. The understanding of this detail and the working knowledge of how to follow the information you uncover is all part of this profession.

Be discreet when meeting clients. Meet away from their home or office address. If you are meeting in a public place be aware of who is sitting near to you. Are they within hearing range? Are they sitting alone and therefore more likely to tune into your conversation? Discretion and privacy are vital.

If you want to get into this business but do not want to start your own company there is always the option of becoming a freelance investigator. Good PI Agencies are always looking for assistance with projects and many work with freelancers for a wide variety of reasons.

A PI does not need a commercial office to work effectively. During startup keeping costs down will be important. Take time to judge your needs as you build your business. If it is a decision between investing in office space and say joining a networking organisation work out which one will help your business most at that point. If and when you decide office space is required take time to look at all options e.g. serviced offices could be a good starting solution where you can get a short letting period with fixed costs.

If you decide that you are going to work from home, you should consider renting a serviced office 'virtual' address for marketing and correspondence purposes. In the PI business it is never a good idea to advertise your home address. You should note that it is fairly straightforward to identify the address behind a PO Box number and technically providing such an address may not be acceptable for certain purposes.

PO Box?

Understand that what your client says they want may be different from what they actually need to achieve the end result. You must remain emotionally detached from your clients case and from the outset be analytical in your assessment of the most likley outcome. Do not, under any circumstances take on work which is beyond your expertise or which you know will not succeed regardless of the money you might earn.

While you can develop your ability for recall there is no substitute for taking notes and a pen and paper will rarely let you down so make sure they are part of your kit. Using technology to record notes is fine but whatever you use be disciplined and ensure you store your written notes, dictated recordings or video safely and securely.

If you are due to go somewhere for the first time, what do you know about the area? Is it somehwere you know well? Is it a well attended public place during daylight or some quiet corner of an empty car park late at night? Be aware of your surroundings, plan ahead but be prepared to reassess the situation at any given moment.

Don't be tempted to believe all you are being told. Question everything that you don't understand and especially that which appears impossible, it usually is. Learn to read body language but try not to confuse the other persons nervousness for anything other than what it is.

Don't set out to buy every 'spy gadget' on the market, apart from the cost the chances are you won't need them and they often don't work in the way they are marketed. Also, bear in mind that buying them may be legal but using them may not. As with every aspect of your work understand the law or consult with someone who does.

An issue with being a Private Investigator is that too many people have seen too many films and TV shows that give a completely misleading impression as to what we do and some have expectations of us that go beyond the law. To stay on the safe side first consider 'hacking' and 'blagging' as illegal... don't do it.

7 in UK Court Over Phone Hacking

...Andy Coulson, who edited the News of the World tabloid before joining Prime Minister David Cameron next court appearance was set for....

Using keystroke spyware on a personal PC, laptop or similar device not used by your client is illegal under The Computer Misuse and Cybercrime Act.

GPS trackers are excellent alternatives to manned surveillance as they can save the client money and time while allowing you to work on more than one case. It may be that you use these devices for preliminary tracking while honing down the case to visual identification if needed using conventional surveillance techniques.

Using a tracker on a vehicle not being used, owned or registered to the client could be viewed as a breach of The Human Rights Act. Maintaining information from a tracking device comes under The Data Protection Act. Following a common thread throughout this book... *if in doubt seek legal guidance*!

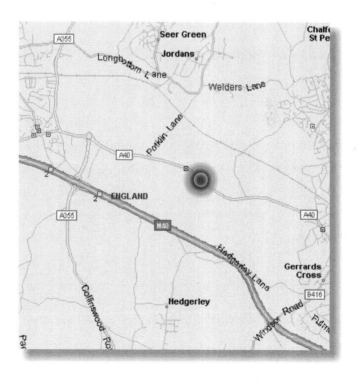

One person carrying out surveillance is not recommended even for an experienced investigator. While circumstances may dictate otherwise a minimum of two people is best practice. If using vehicles make sure they are of different makes and colours and as low key as possible. Following a target in your shiny red Ferrari could be a little too conspicuous.

Surveillance, especially moving surveillance, is not an exact science. You can perform the tasks under agreed upon time and location parameters but you cannot control what the subject of your enquiries does or the state of traffic and road conditions on the day. If it is going against you, stop the operation, regroup and resume at another time. Better to back off than risk being spotted or committing a traffic violation.

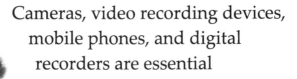

Cameras, video recording devices, mobile phones, and digital recorders are essential equipment to be able to obtain and record intelligence you need, just make sure you use them within the bounds of the law. And...don't forget to charge the batteries before each job, if in doubt carry secondary equipment and back up batteries.

Learn how to use all of your equipment properly. Don't wait until they are needed before you read the manual. Using the tools of your trade should be second nature and practice makes perfect; practice in your time not that of your client. When it comes to the point of using the kit in the field you will be able to focus on the matter in hand rather than fumbling for the on switch.

Depending on the area of the world in which you operate you may have to consider time zones when setting up equipment. For instance, if you are in the UK don't forget to reset the clock in your camera when British summer time begins and ends. You do not want digital time recording to conflict with any reports you make.

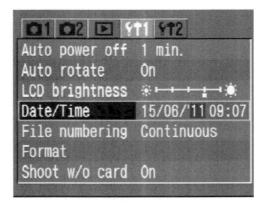

For close surveillance, invest in mini body/covert cameras and recording devices but always research and try before buying. If possible ask other PI's for their opinion.

If a lot of the work you intend to do will include a high degree of surveillance invest in a van or vehicle that is custom made for the job or can easily be converted for the purpose. Either way use black tint on your vehicle windows to help avoid detection.

At the outset cultivate law firm clients who will give you regular Process Serving work. This initial business could be your bread and butter revenue stream and will help you establish your credibility with the legal profession.

Matrimonial Surveillance on cheating partners is not as profitable or as attractive work as some may think and usually, by its very nature, does not generate much referred business. Corporate and commercial investigations are generally more lucrative and have the added advantage of generating repeat work as well as better sources of referrals.

Dress according to your surroundings e.g., don't wear an old track suit in an up-market area or a designer business suit where it will make you stand out like a sore thumb. You must blend in or risk detection by your target.

Wherever you are working a surveillance operation always have an exit route planned and a plausible story prepared in case you are questioned.

Advertising your services as a PI can be a costly excercise with often little or no return for your investment. Invest first in joining a networking group in your area such as BNI - your visibility and credibility will increase faster among the local business community. Referral or word of mouth marketing is by far the best way to generate business. Important: *referred business comes fastest to the person who refers first.* Make sure you are constantly looking for ways to refer to others especially to your clients.

Look at completing Road Traffic Accident Investigation and Interview Technique courses. This will bring additional work from insurance related investigation claims.

Law firms specialising in areas such as personal injury work will often sub-contract the taking of witness statements which can add to your to your service offering. If its a skill set which you need to acquire there are courses available but make sure they are provided by those with a proven track record in this area of training.

A good investigator establishes a network of trusted contacts who can supply information as and when required. This may include other investigators who will often share information among colleagues once credibility and trust have been established. Build and look after your network and it will look after you.

The internet is a PI's major resource for local and global information so learn to get the best from your browser. Much of the work you will do will be research across the web. Start building your own library of source information, data and contacts. Remember, information is your stock in trade.

When carrying out tracing on individuals, remember to follow up with discreet enquiries in the area to confirm residency. The latest result on a tracing database may not be the most up to date so always look for ways to confirm the information you may have.

Make yourself fully aware of the provisions of the UK Data Protection Act (or similar depending on the country you are in) and adhere to its principles. If in doubt consult an expert in that area of law.

If in the UK, one of the first things you should do is register with the Information Commissioners Office under the current Data Protection Act.

Information Commissioner's Office

Invest in the professional services needed to support you. The best accountant, lawyer and business coach will be worth every penny they charge by bringing their experience to your business and they will always look for ways to refer business to you - in fact you should make that part of the measure of their support.

If you are hiring a business coach or mentor there are some questions you should ask before you make your decision - 1. Have they created a successful business from scratch; 2. Are they independent or part of a franchise where one size might fit all; 3. Can they provide 3 references to clients they have helped; 4. Can they refer work to you.

When calculating your hourly investigation fees include all your costs - travel time, research, reporting time, fuel, insurance etc. If you are working from home factor in the cost as if it were rented offices; lease, electricity, heating...You need to price your services with profit in mind, remember its a business not a hobby.

It is good business practice to obtain indemnity and liability insurance so make sure you are fully covered. A good insurance broker will guide you.

You are not just an investigator, first and foremost you own a business. Write a business plan, prepare proper accounts, develop a marketing strategy. Learn negotiation and presentation skills and use them to discuss fees, be prepared to be flexible but do not sell yourself short.

Talk to other investigators in your area. They will often be happy to give work on an agent to agent basis and they might specialise in areas of which you do not have knowledge, e.g. digital forensics and tracing; it can be a great way to gain exposure to new skills.

Don't turn down profitable work, establish a reputation as a 'can do' agency. If you can't carry out the task, either enlist the assistance of or sub contract the work to an agency who can do it.

It's good to gain a basic knowledge of the broader sweep of law - in the UK that might include Regulation of Investigatory Powers Act, Human Rights Act, and Criminal Procedure & Investigations Act. Also be aware of changes to the laws. But remember, these laws are complex, it can take years for legal professionals to understand them and importantly how the various laws may interplay.

When conducting surveillance in a residential area inform the police of your presence. It would not be the first time an investigator has been observed in a car for long periods and presumed to be someone up to no good.

Stick to your morals, principles and the ethics of business. Don't stray from the right path, never let hard cash persuade you into accepting illegal activities.

Have someone you know on speed
dial with whom you can maintain
contact if needed. If you are working
in 'hostile' areas perhaps late at night,
tell someone where you will be and
give them a time you will call in.
Personal safety has to be a priority for
you and your team.

Study body language. Learn to read others from the way they move, stand, sit, walk, fold their arms, touch their face etc., they may well give you more information about themselves than through the words they use. Add NLP to your study topics, the more you practice techniques of observation the more second nature it will become.

It is better not to
carry weapons of
any kind, even if
the laws of
your
country
permit you
to. Develop
the skill to talk
your way out of
situations, think
on your feet but
be prepared to
use them to walk
away or run should
you have to.

In some cases it is more productive not tell anyone that you are an investigator and in order to get the job done you may need to assume a role. If that is the case, do not overcomplicate it, prepare well and use the role to observe more than to participate.

Investigators will often work in teams or, subject to circumstances, alone. You must be able to adapt to work in any situation and be able to work without supervision.

You will find some surveillance long, boring and tiring and sometimes it may seem pointless. You must have a long attention span, the ability to keep alert and always be thinking one step ahead of the situation.

Providing a quality service will bring quality clients and you are more likley to be given repeat work as well as be referred to others. Set your client care standards as high as possible, strive to be the best in the business.

And...

...enjoy it. Love what you are doing. Have the best interest of your client as the centre piece of your work and feel privileged that you have a role that can be different every day. Celebrate the success you create and enjoy the rewards of that success. Be a brilliant Private Investigator.

2400939R00034

Printed in Great Britain
by Amazon.co.uk, Ltd.,
Marston Gate.